My Home
Hong Kong

Donna Bailey and Jeremy Taylor

M
MACMILLAN EDUCATION

Hello! My name is Lee Sin-Kai.
I live in Hong Kong.
Hong Kong is very close to China.
It has a big island called
Hong Kong Island, lots of other islands
and a part of the mainland.

One of my uncles lives on the mainland
in a place called the New Territories.
I live on the mainland too in a place
called Kowloon.

In the summer Hong Kong is very hot.
It rains a lot and everyone has to carry
an umbrella.
The rain goes on for days and days.

4

Sometimes we get very strong winds
called typhoons.
Then everyone has to stay inside.
The typhoon usually lasts one or two days.
It can do a lot of damage to
the houses and buildings.

Hong Kong is a very small place but
lots of people live there.
There is very little land to build houses
so most people live in flats.
I live in a small flat with my family.

People living in flats do not have
their own gardens.
They use the balconies of their flats
to hang their washing out and
they grow plants there.

Kowloon has many markets and big shops
as well as flats.
Tourists like to buy goods in these shops.
You can also buy little snacks from
the food stalls in the street.

Sometimes I go to visit my aunt on
Hong Kong Island.
We go to the Island by ferry.
A ferry goes from Kowloon every
five minutes all day long.

My aunt lives in a place called Aberdeen.
We take a very old tram from near the ferry.
Then we catch a bus to Aberdeen.

My aunt lives in Aberdeen harbour on
a large boat called a junk.
When we arrive at the harbour she meets us
and takes us on her sampan to her home.

A sampan is a little boat.
It has a cover to keep the rain off.
Some people row their sampans, but
my aunt's sampan has an engine.
She goes quite fast through the water.
We soon arrive at her junk.

My aunt keeps chickens and her dog
on the junk.
When she wants to go shopping or
visit her friends, she uses her sampan.
Traders also come in their boats
to sell her vegetables and fruit.

My uncle is a fisherman.
In the morning he takes the junk
to join the fishing fleet.
My aunt, my cousins, the chickens and
the dog all go in the junk with him.

14

My uncle sells the fish he has caught
in the fish market.
People in Hong Kong love eating fresh fish.
They buy most of their food from markets.

Index